Practical
Pre-School

Planning
for Learning
through

The Twelve Days
of Christmas

Rachel Sparks Linfield and Penny Coltman   Illustrated by Cathy Hughes

Contents

Published by Step Forward Publishing Limited
Coach House, Cross Road, Milverton, Leamington Spa, CV32 5PB   Tel: 01926 420046
© Step Forward Publishing Limited 2000
Planning for Learning through The Twelve Days of Christmas   ISBN: 1-902438-25-6

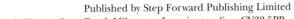

MAKING PLANS

WHY PLAN?

The purpose of planning is to make sure that all children enjoy a broad and balanced curriculum. All planning should be useful. Plans are working documents which you spend time preparing, but which should later repay your efforts. Try to be concise. This will help you in finding information quickly when you need it.

LONG-TERM PLANS

Preparing a long-term plan, which maps out the curriculum during a year or even two, will help you to ensure that you are providing a variety of activities and are meeting statutory requirements of the Early Learning Goals (1999).

Your long-term plan need not be detailed. Divide the time period over which you are planning into fairly equal sections, such as half terms. Choose a topic for each section. Young children benefit from making links between the new ideas they encounter so as you select each topic, think about the time of year in which you plan to do it. A topic about minibeasts will not be very successful in November!

Although each topic will address all the learning areas, some could focus on a specific area. For example, a topic on Spring would lend itself well to activities relating to knowledge and understanding of the living world. Another topic might particularly encourage the appreciation of stories. Try to make sure that you provide a variety of topics in your long-term plans.

Autumn 1	All about me
Autumn 2	Autumn Christmas
Spring 1	Fairy stories
Spring 2	Changes
Summer 1	Toys
Summer 2	Out and about

MEDIUM-TERM PLANS

Medium-term plans will outline the contents of a topic in a little more detail. One way to start this process is by brainstorming on a large piece of paper. Work with your team writing down all the activities you can think of which are relevant to the topic. As you do this it may become clear that some activities go well together. Think about dividing them into themes. The topic of Christmas, for example, has themes such as Advent, the Christmas story and Christmas presents.

At this stage it is helpful to make a chart. Write the theme ideas down the side of the chart and put a different area of learning at the top of each column. Now you can insert your brainstormed ideas and will quickly see where there are gaps. As you complete the chart take account of children's earlier experiences and provide opportunities for them to progress.

Refer back to the Early Learning Goals and check that you have addressed as many different aspects of it as you can. Once all your medium-term plans are complete make sure that there are no neglected areas.

MAKING PLANS

DAY-TO-DAY PLANS

The plans you make for each day will outline aspects such as:

- resources needed;
- the way in which you might introduce activities;
- the organisation of adult help;
- size of the group;
- timing.

Identify the learning which each activity is intended to promote. Make a note of any assessments or observations which you are likely to carry out. On your plans make notes of which activities were particularly successful, or any changes you would make another time.

A FINAL NOTE

Planning should be seen as flexible. Not all groups meet every day, and not all children attend every day. Any part of the plans in this book can be used independently, stretched over a longer period or condensed to meet the needs of any group. You will almost certainly adapt the activities as children respond to them in different ways and bring their own ideas, interests and enthusiasms. Be prepared to be flexible over timing as some ideas prove more popular than others. The important thing is to ensure that the children are provided with a varied and enjoyable curriculum which meets their individual developing needs.

USING THE BOOK:

- Collect or prepare suggested resources as listed on page 21.

- Read the section which outlines links to the Early Learning Goals (pages 4 - 7) and explains the rationale for the topic of Christmas.

- This book covers a twelve-day period. It is divided into six themes, each of which presents activities for a two-day period. It is suggested that you might carry out the activities relating to Advent during the last two working days of November. This will allow the children, for example, to make a group Advent calendar. The other 'themes' would then be carried out during the final ten days of the term.

- For each theme two activities are described in detail as an example to help you in your planning and preparation. Key vocabulary, questions and learning opportunities are identified.

- The skills chart on page 23 will help you to see at a glance which aspects of children's development are being addressed as a focus each day.

- As children take part in the Christmas topic activities, their learning will progress. 'Collecting evidence' on page 22 explains how you might monitor children's achievements.

- Find out on page 20 how the topic can be brought together in a grand finale involving parents, children and friends.

- There is additional material to support the working partnership of families and children in the form of a 'Home links' page, and a photocopiable parent's page found at the back of the book.

It is important to appreciate that the ideas presented in this book will only be a part of your planning. Many activities which will be taking place as routine in your group may not be mentioned. For example, it is assumed that sand, dough, water, puzzles, floor toys and large scale apparatus are part of the ongoing pre-school experience. More and more groups are also able to offer opportunities for children to develop ICT skills. Role-play areas, stories, rhymes and singing, and group discussion times are similarly assumed to be happening as well, although they may not be a focus for described activities.

Note: Whilst Christmas is a Christian celebration, it is important that children from other cultural backgrounds enjoy and understand the activities. For these children Christmas provides a context within which activities relating to the Early Learning Goals are placed. Equally, festivals from other world religions practised by families of children within the group should be given prominence at appropriate times during the year.

USING THE EARLY LEARNING GOALS

Having decided on your topic and made your medium-term plans you can use the Early Learning Goals to highlight the key learning opportunities your activities will address. The goals are split into six areas: Personal, Social and Emotional Development, Language and Literacy, Mathematical Development, Knowledge and Understanding of the World, Physical Development and Creative Development. Do not expect each of your topics to cover every goal but your long-term plans should allow for each child to work towards all of the goals.

The following section highlights parts of the Early Learning Goals document in point form to show what children are expected to be able to do by the time they enter Year 1 in each area of learning. These points will be used throughout this book to show how activities for a topic on Christmas link to these expectations. For example, Language and Literacy point 2 is 'explore and experiment with sounds, words and texts'. Activities suggested which provide the opportunity for children to do this will have the reference L2. This will enable you to see which parts of the Early Learning Goals are covered in a given week and plan for areas to be revisited and developed.

In addition you can ensure that activities offer variety in the outcomes to be encountered. Often a similar activity may be carried out to achieve different learning outcomes. For example, during this topic children make their own Christmas cards. They will be learning about materials as they make and describe their choices of decoration, discovering aspects of technology as they fold the card and using early literacy skills as they write their messages inside.

It is important therefore that activities have clearly defined learning outcomes so that these may be emphasised during the activity and for recording purposes.

PERSONAL, SOCIAL AND EMOTIONAL DEVELOPMENT (PS)

This area of learning covers important aspects of development which affect the way children learn, behave and relate to others.

By the end of the foundation stage most children will:

PS1   continue to be interested, excited and motivated to learn

PS2   be confident to try new activities, initiate ideas and speak in a familiar group

PS3   maintain attention, concentrate and sit quietly when appropriate

PS4   have a developing awareness of their own needs, views and feelings and be sensitive to the needs, views and feelings of others

PS5   have a developing respect for their own cultures and beliefs and those of other people

PS6   respond to significant experiences, showing a range of feelings when appropriate

PS7   form good relationships with adults and peers

PS8 work as a part of a group or class, taking turns and sharing fairly; understanding that there need to be agreed values and codes of behaviour for groups of people, including adults and children, to work together harmoniously

PS9 understand what is right, what is wrong and why

PS10 dress and undress independently and manage their own personal hygiene

PS11 select and use activities and resources independently

PS12 consider the consequences of their words and actions for themselves and others

PS13 understand that people have different needs, views, cultures and beliefs which need to be treated with respect

PS14 understand that they can expect others to treat their needs, views, cultures and beliefs with respect

The topic of Christmas provides valuable opportunities for children to develop an awareness of the cultures and traditions associated with this time of year. They will be able to work as a group being sensitive to the needs and feelings of others. Many outcomes will also develop as a natural result of activities in other key areas. For example, when children play dice games within Mathematical Development they will also have the opportunity to further PS8.

LANGUAGE AND LITERACY (L)

The objectives set out in the *National literacy strategy: Framework for teaching* for the reception year are in line with these goals. By the end of the foundation stage, most children will be able to:

Children will:

L1 enjoy listening to and using spoken and written language, and readily turn to it in their play and learning

L2 explore and experiment with sounds, words and texts

L3 listen with enjoyment and respond to stories, songs and other music, rhymes and poems and make up their own stories, songs, rhymes and poems

L4 use language to imagine and recreate roles and experiences

L5 use talk to organise, sequence and clarify thinking, ideas, feelings and events

L6 sustain attentive listening, responding to what they have heard by relevant comments, questions or actions

L7 interact with others, negotiating plans and activities and taking turns in conversation

L8 extend their vocabulary, exploring the meaning and sounds of new words

L9 retell narratives in the correct sequence, drawing on the language patterns of stories

L10 speak clearly and audibly with confidence and control and show awareness of the listener, for example by their use of conventions such as greetings, 'please' and 'thank you'

L11 hear and say initial and final sounds in words and short vowel sounds within words

L12 link sounds to letters, naming and sounding the letters of the alphabet

L13 read a range of familiar and common words and simple sentences independently

L14 show an understanding of the elements of stories such as main character, sequence of events, and opening and how information can be found in non-fiction texts to answer questions about where, who, why and how

L15 know that print carries meaning and, in English, is read from left to right and top to bottom

L16 attempt writing for various purposes, using features of different forms such as lists, stories and instructions

L17 write their own names, labels and captions, and begin to form sentences, sometimes using punctuation

L18 use their phonic knowledge to write simple regular words and make phonetically plausible attempts at more complex words

L19 use a pencil and hold it effectively to form recognisable letters, most of which are correctly formed

The activities suggested for the theme of Christmas provide the opportunity for children to respond to stories and to participate in role play. The writing of name labels for party bags and filling stockings with words or pictures will help children to develop their early writing skills. Writing and investigating the greetings in Christmas cards will help children to know that words carry meaning and therefore give

purpose
to their own writing.
Throughout all the activities
children will be encouraged to communicate
fluently with meaning.

MATHEMATICAL DEVELOPMENT (M)

These goals cover important aspects of mathematical understanding and provide the foundation for numeracy. They focus on achievement through practical activities and on using and understanding language in the development of simple mathematical ideas.

The key objectives in the *National numeracy strategy: Framework for teaching* for the reception year are in line with these goals. By the end of the foundation stage, most children will be able to:

M1   say and use number names in order in familiar contexts

M2   count reliably up to ten everyday objects

M3   recognise numerals 1 to 9

M4   use language such as 'more' or 'less', 'greater' or 'smaller', 'heavier' or 'lighter' to compare two numbers or quantities

M5   in practical activities and discussion begin to use the vocabulary involved in adding and subtracting

M6   find one more or one less than a number from one to ten

M7   begin to relate addition to combining two groups of objects and subtraction to 'taking away'

M8   talk about, recognise and recreate simple patterns

M9   use language such as 'circle' or 'bigger' to describe the shape and size of solids and flat shapes

M10   use everyday words to describe position

M11   use developing mathematical ideas and methods to solve practical problems

During the activities suggested in this Christmas work, children will explore several aspects of shape and pattern. Sorting, matching and making Christmas cards and making tree decorations give experience of 2D shapes, and investigating and describing parcels extends familiarity with shapes that have three dimensions. Printing wrapping paper and making paper chains are used to give experience of copying, continuing and making repeating patterns. Counting is a continuing theme throughout as children develop confidence in number names and order.

KNOWLEDGE AND UNDERSTANDING OF THE WORLD (K)

By the end of the foundation stage, most children will be able to:

K1   investigate objects and materials by using all of their senses as appropriate

K2   find out about and identify some features of living things, objects and events they observe

K3   look closely at similarities, differences, patterns and change

K4   ask questions about why things happen and how things work

K5   build and construct with a wide range of objects, selecting appropriate resources and adapting their work where necessary

K6   select tools and techniques they need to shape, assemble and join the materials they are using

K7   find out about and identify the uses of everyday technology and use information and communication technology and programmable toys to support their learning

K8   find out about past and present events in their own lives, and in those of their families and other people they know

K9   observe, find out about and identify features in the place they live and the natural world

K10   begin to know about their own cultures and beliefs and those of other people

K11   find out about their environment and talk about those features they like and dislike

The topic of Christmas provides an opportunity to help children experience goals K1 to K9. In particular, as they work to produce decorations, cards and presents, they will be able to explore materials and to enjoy cutting, folding and gluing. Within all their work children should be encouraged to talk about their observations and to consider similarities, differences, pattern and change.

PHYSICAL DEVELOPMENT (PD)

By the end of the foundation stage most children will be able to:

PD1   move with confidence, imagination and in safety

PD2   move with control and co-ordination

PD3   show awareness of space, of themselves and of others

PD4   recognise the importance of keeping healthy and those things which contribute to this

PD5   recognise the changes that happen to their bodies when they are active

PD6   use a range of small and large equipment

PD7   travel around, under, over and through balancing and climbing equipment

PD8   handle tools, objects, construction and malleable materials safely and with increasing control

Activities such as the cracker game and the shepherd and wolves game will encourage children to move with co-ordination, imagination and control. Through working as a whole group children will become aware of the restrictions of space and the needs of others. Games such as tree skittles and aiming bean bags into Christmas boxes will encourage children to use small apparatus with increasing skill.

CREATIVE DEVELOPMENT (C)

By the end of the foundation stage, most children will be able to:

C1   explore colour, texture, shape, form and space in two and three dimensions

C2   recognise and explore how sounds can be changed, sing simple songs from memory, recognise repeated sounds and sound patterns and match movements to music

C3   respond in a variety of ways to what they see, hear, smell, touch and feel

C4   use their imagination in art and design, music, dance, imaginative and role play and stories

C5   express and communicate their ideas, thoughts and feelings by using a widening range of materials, suitable tools, imaginative and role play, movement, designing and making, and a variety of songs and musical instruments

During this topic children will experience working with a variety of materials as they make collage presents, decorations and cards. Through using decorations, Christmas stamps and old Christmas cards they will be able to explore colour and respond to what they see, touch and feel. The use of finger puppets to enact the Christmas story will allow children to use their imaginations, to listen and to observe. Stories throughout the topic provide a key stimulus for listening, looking and responding.

DAYS 1 AND 2

ADVENT

You need to plan to make the Advent calendar at the end of November so that the first door can be opened on 1st December

PERSONAL, SOCIAL AND EMOTIONAL DEVELOPMENT

- Discuss Advent as the time approaches Christmas. Talk about how children prepare for Christmas with their families. Explain that some people do not celebrate Christmas and that some celebrate different festivals. Draw on children from the group who can talk about festivals from other world religions. (PS4, 5)

LANGUAGE AND LITERACY

- On a large sheet of paper draw a Christmas tree. Explain that over the next two weeks the group is going to make a collection of Christmas words. On bauble shaped pieces of paper scribe for the children words they suggest to do with Christmas and stick them on the tree. (L8)

- Make a Santa's workshop role-play area. (L1, 4)

MATHEMATICAL DEVELOPMENT

- Look at Advent candles. Count the rings. From paper make a large candle for the number of days until the holidays. Each day cut off one segment and count how many remain. (M1, 2, 5)

- Play a simple dice game in which counters are moved along a candle-shaped number track to reach the flame. Encourage children to recognise the number on the die and to count out loud as they move their counter. (M1, 2)

KNOWLEDGE AND UNDERSTANDING OF THE WORLD

- Make Christmas wreath decorations. Prepare bases by cutting the centres from large card circles. Supply leaves and small fir cones to decorate. Discuss the materials as the children use them to decorate their wreaths. Supply red ribbon bows to add the finishing touch. (K2, 5,)

PHYSICAL DEVELOPMENT

- Play a counting movement game in which children do one jump, two hops, three strides, four .... Depending upon children's knowledge of numbers the game can be played up to 24. Invite children to make suggestions for the movements. (PD1, 2)

CREATIVE DEVELOPMENT

- Make a large group Advent calendar which might involve several notice boards. The calendar should include items which can be removed each day (stars, snowballs) and could contain small surprises for the children (for example chocolate pennies, stickers). Effective calendars are:

A snow scene where each child makes a snowman or person for the calendar. The doors are white circles - snowballs. The scene could be based on a *Where's Wally?* type picture in which all the people are dressed in clothes of similar colours. Each day, as well as looking for the 'door', children could be encouraged to spot Wally who should be moved before the children arrive and who does not always need to be on the calendar! (C1)

A scene depicting a shiny red post-box, envelopes and Christmas stamps. (C1)

A traditional Bethlehem manger scene. This could either be silhouettes from black paper, which includes stars made by the children, or a 3D manger in which children make the characters from plastic bottles, fabrics, wool or paper and stand them in front of a star frieze. (C1)

ACTIVITY: Post-box CD. Advent calendar

Learning opportunity: Exploring the colours and pictures on postage stamps. Making stamps for the group Advent calendar.

Early Learning Goal: Creative Development. Children will explore colour in two dimensions.

Resources: A collection of envelopes numbered from

1 to 24; paper cut into stamp shapes with pinking shears; crayons, felt pens and pencils; glue; a cut-out of a large, shiny, red post-box mounted on a wintry display scene; examples of Christmas edition stamps (postcards of stamps are ideal as they can be viewed by the whole group at once); an example of an Advent calendar.

Organisation: Whole group.

Key vocabulary: Days, weeks, months.

WHAT TO DO:

Show the group an Advent calendar. Talk about what it is used for. Explain that the group is going to make an Advent calendar. Show the children the post-box display and the envelopes. Explain how the envelopes are numbered, and that one is going to be opened each day until Christmas.

Invite the children to make Christmas stamps to go on the envelopes. What makes a stamp eye catching? What colours are 'Christmassy'? Show children examples of real stamps.

Give each child a stamp shaped piece of paper to decorate. Encourage children to do several and to pick their favourite for the calendar. (Spare stamps can be kept for envelopes for cards children make before the end of the term.)After the children have gone home you can place a surprise in each envelope.

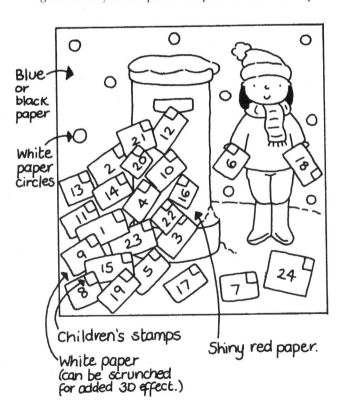

Blue or black paper

White paper circles

Children's stamps

White paper (can be scrunched for added 3D effect.)

Shiny red paper.

The envelopes can then be stapled across one corner onto and cascading from the post-box.

ACTIVITY: Santa's workshop role-play area   L+L

Learning opportunity: Developing and discussing imaginative ideas as children work together in constructing a role-play area.

Early Learning Goal: Language and Literacy. Children will use language to imagine and recreate roles.

Resources: Two tables; safe scissors; glue or sticky tape; a collection of glittery papers; boxes; recycled materials; decorative materials; note pads and pencils; a world map; toy or Christmas shopping catalogues.

Organisation: Involve as many children as possible in assembling the area, a few at a time.

WHAT TO DO:

Explain to the children that together they are going to make a Christmas workshop. They will be able to pretend to be Father Christmas and his helpers. They have so many toys to make for delivery - the weeks before Christmas will be quite hectic!

Involve the children in equipping a workbench with tools and resources for making things. Encourage the children to offer ideas. What would Santa need?

Talk about how children write to Santa with their Christmas requests. Invite the 'writing' of order forms by adding notepads, pencils and a couple of covered shoe boxes labelled 'In tray' and 'Work done'.

Finishing touches might include a route map on the wall, pictures of reindeer, toy catalogues to act as sources of inspiration (for making and writing), a delivery sack and one or two elfin hats.

DISPLAY

Mount the tree made in the first Language and Literacy activity at floor level near the role-play area. Encourage children to add decorations to the tree over the coming days. On a table start a display of favourite Christmas picture books.

DAYS 3 AND 4

CHRISTMAS DECORATIONS

PERSONAL, SOCIAL AND EMOTIONAL DEVELOPMENT

- Use the story of 'The Smallest Tree' (in which it is the smallest tree which is chosen to be a Christmas tree) to discuss the importance of treating others with sensitivity and appreciating that everyone has special qualities to contribute. (PS2, 4)

LANGUAGE AND LITERACY

- Discuss the party which will be held on the last day of term. Decorate letters to parents requesting food for the party. (L16)

- Make name labels to be attached to individual party bags for each child at the party. (L16)

- Read *The Little Christ Child and the Spiders* by Jan Peters (Macdonald), in which tinsel is likened to a spider's web, or a tale of how Christmas trees came to be. (L3)

MATHEMATICAL DEVELOPMENT

- Encourage children to sort paper shapes into circles, triangles and squares. Use the shapes to make decorations to hang on the tree started in the Advent sessions. (M9)

- Make paper chains using strips of sticky paper which are based upon repeating patterns such as red, yellow, green, red, yellow, green. Some of the chains can be used to decorate the room and also the role play area.(M8)

KNOWLEDGE AND UNDERSTANDING OF THE WORLD

- Ask children to help Santa to sort a range of materials for use in making decorations - see activity right. (K1, 3)

- Talk about the Christmas decorations which children have seen in supermarkets, shopping centres, or perhaps street lights. Encourage the children to express ideas and preferences, and to compare different displays they have seen. (K11)

PHYSICAL DEVELOPMENT

- Play the cracker game (see activity opposite). (PD1, 2, 3)

- Make and use Christmas tree skittles from plastic bottles and crepe paper. (PD6)

CREATIVE DEVELOPMENT

- Unpack a box of favourite decorations (a shiny bauble, wooden angel, small bear). Discuss with children what makes the decorations special. Encourage children to choose one and to make up a story about it. (C3, 4)

- Make stars from card and shiny materials to hang from the ceiling. (C1)

ACTIVITY: Sorting materials for Father Christmas

KUW.

Learning opportunity: Sorting materials according to properties such as shiny, paper, fabric.

Early Learning Goal: Knowledge and Understanding of the World. Children will look closely at similarities and differences.

Resources: a mixed collection of scraps of shiny materials, fabrics, papers; glue; scissors; A4 card cut out into tree, star and stocking shapes; letter from Father Christmas.

Organisation: Whole group introduction, up to six children on the practical activity.

Key vocabulary: Shiny, dull, smooth, rough.

1 Snowy Street
Lapland

Dear Children,
I am in deep trouble. Rudolph my reindeer sneezed and has muddled up all the materials I use to make decorations. Also, my helpers have got the flu and cannot do any work at the moment. Please can you help me to sort the materials and to make some decorations? I enclose some card decorations. Please could you cover the stars with shiny scraps, the trees with paper scraps and the stockings with fabric?

Lots of love,
from Father Christmas

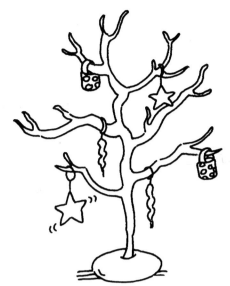

WHAT TO DO:

Show and read to the group a letter from Father Christmas (see above).

Show the group the muddled materials. Ask the children to identify a piece of fabric. Ask for words to describe it. Talk about the colour and the texture.

Identify papers and then shiny materials. Discuss the fact that some materials may fit into more than one category (for example, shiny paper).

Explain that the group is going to help Father Christmas. Give pairs of children a tree, stocking or star. Remind them of the type of material they should look for. Encourage the children to cover their decoration and to find as many different examples of the property as they can.

ACTIVITY: The cracker game P.D.

Learning opportunity: Moving imaginatively, within a group, in a large space.

Early Learning Goal: Physical Development. Children will move with confidence, imagination and in safety, and move with control and co-ordination.

Resources: A cassette player and some seasonal music.

Organisation: Whole group.

WHAT TO DO:

This game is a variation on a tried and tested theme. Explain to the children that they are going to move around the room to music, skipping, walking, hopping, etc. When the music stops, call out a Christmas word. Each word tells the children to do something different. Examples might include:

Christmas pudding: Make a small round shape.

Holly leaves : Make a spiky shape.

Christmas candle: Make a tall shape, waving arms above head to form a 'flame.'

Father Christmas: Pretend to deliver parcels.

Christmas Eve: Pretend to be asleep.

Christmas cracker: The favourite! Crouch, then jump in the air, clapping hands.

DISPLAY

Collect a small twiggy branch fallen from a tree. Spray it with white paint.

Cut a long slice (about 1 cm thick) from one side of a very large baking potato. The potato should now rest securely on a flat surface. Cover it with cooking foil. The covered potato is now a firm base into which the end of the branch can be pushed.

Invite the children to use paper, sequins, foils and other light materials to produce decorations of their own designs to hang on the little winter tree.

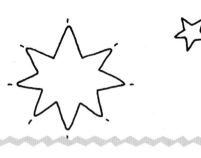

DAYS 5 AND 6

THE CHRISTMAS STORY

PERSONAL, SOCIAL AND EMOTIONAL DEVELOPMENT

- Retell or read a simple version of the Christmas story. Discuss what it might have been like to be one of the people in the story (Joseph - anxious, shepherd - scared, angel - excited). (PS2, 4)

LANGUAGE AND LITERACY

- Encourage children to retell the Christmas story by using a picture book such as *The First Christmas* retold by Lynne Bradbury (Ladybird). (L9)

- Read *Jesus' Christmas Party* by Nicholas Allan. Use it as the stimulus for role play. (L1, 3)

MATHEMATICAL DEVELOPMENT

- On a piece of A4 paper provide children with pictures from the Christmas story to show numbers 1 to 10 (for example 1 star, 2 shepherds, 3 wise men, 4 cows ....10 angels). The pictures should be coloured, cut out and then stuck on a strip of paper in number order. (M1, 2, 3)

- Use the following number rhyme. Encourage children to invent actions to depict the characters in the rhyme and to represent the number with their fingers. (M1)

One star shining bright,

Two travellers in the night.

Three wise men from far away,

Four donkeys munching hay.

Five shepherds in a row,

Six sheep as white as snow.

Seven angels join to sing,

Happy Birthday to our King.

KNOWLEDGE AND UNDERSTANDING OF THE WORLD

- The shepherds and wise men travelled a long way following the Christmas star. Invite the children to talk about long journeys they have made. These might include visits to relatives and friends, exciting days out or holiday trips. (K8)

- Christmas winding (see activity opposite). (K5)

PHYSICAL DEVELOPMENT

- Play the 'Shepherds and wolves' game (see activity opposite). (PD2, 3)

CREATIVE DEVELOPMENT

- Sing Christmas songs about the Christmas story. (C2)

- Cut out pictures from Christmas cards and glue them onto small paper bands to make simple finger puppets. Use them to enact the Christmas story. (C4)

ACTIVITY: Christmas winding KUW.

Learning opportunity: Exploring and comparing materials.

Early Learning Goal: Knowledge and Understanding of the World. Children will select appropriate resources.

Resources: Postcard-sized pieces of black card, cut down the sides using pinking shears; wool, ribbons or raffia; sparkly threads - gold and silver wool with a lurex thread; tinsel; sparkly pipe-cleaners.

Organisation: Small group with adult supervision.

Key vocabulary: Green, red, white, gold, silver.

WHAT TO DO:

Talk to the children about the colours associated with Christmas - the greens of the Christmas trees or holly leaves, the reds of candles, holly berries or robins, the white of snow, or the gold and silver of decorations.

Explain that they are going to make some wool windings to show these Christmas colours. Let each child choose their own colours.

Help them to start their windings by tying the end of chosen thread around one end of their card. As they change colours, new threads can be tied to the end of the one in use. Show the children how to start winding at one end of the card and gradually fill it as they work to the other end. As the children work, talk about the choices they are making. What does this colour remind you of? Does this wool feel quite the same as that one? Which wool is softer? What does the ribbon feel like?

The finished windings, which will look like simple weaving, should have a variety of shades and textures. Once mounted (which hides the ends) they can be used as Christmas cards, or the basis of a calendar gift.

ACTIVITY: Shepherds and wolves PD.

Learning opportunity: Moving with increasing control.

Early Learning Goal: Physical Development. Children will move with control and co-ordination and awareness of space, themselves and others.

Resources: A large space.

Organisation: Whole group.

Key vocabulary: Wolf, sheep, shepherd, safe, danger.

WHAT TO DO:

Explain that the shepherds in the Nativity were on the hillside looking after their sheep. They needed to make sure that the sheep did not get lost. They also needed to guard them. There were wolves about!

This game is based on 'Grandmother's footsteps'. You are the shepherd, the children are the hungry wolves, trying to creep up silently to steal the sheep.

The wolves start at one end of the hall and you stand at the other with your back to them. Slowly the wolves approach, chanting a rhyme, and stepping in time to the rhythm of the words: 'We are hungry wolves that creep, Looking for a tasty sheep.'

The wolves must watch you carefully because at any time you may turn around. Any wolves seen moving must go back to the beginning. Once a wolf reaches you, use suitably fearsome noises to send the delighted wolves scurrying back to the beginning!

DISPLAY

Display a Nativity scene (bought or made) and encourage children to identify the characters in it. Invite children to add their own made characters and animals to the scene.

DAYS 7 AND 8

CHRISTMAS CARDS

PERSONAL, SOCIAL AND EMOTIONAL DEVELOPMENT

- Provide pairs of children with jigsaws made from old Christmas cards. Encourage them to work collaboratively on the puzzles. (PS8)

LANGUAGE AND LITERACY

- Sort old Christmas cards according to their greetings. Discuss the type of greeting children would like to write in a home-made card. Write the greeting. (L17)

- On large pieces of paper write 'Happy Christmas' in a variety of languages. Show children the greetings. Help them to pronounce the words. Decorate and display them around the room. (L16)

MATHEMATICAL DEVELOPMENT

- Sort old Christmas cards into sets according to the pictures on them (robins, Santa, crib, snowmen). (M11)

- Sort old Christmas cards into sets according to their shapes. (M9, 11)

- Play the Christmas card puzzle game (see activity opposite). (M8, 11)

KNOWLEDGE AND UNDERSTANDING OF THE WORLD

- Make a group Christmas card for anyone who has helped/visited the group over the term. The card should be made using materials of a given property - shiny, soft, smooth. Encourage children to talk about why the material they have chosen is appropriate. (K1, 3, 5)

- Make simple pop-up Christmas cards. (K5)

PHYSICAL DEVELOPMENT

- Play 'Santa's journey'. Make an obstacle course around the room using large apparatus: climbing frame, tunnel, hoops to climb through or step in, stepping stone mats. Place the course within an imaginative Christmas context. As Santa delivers his presents he has to: cross the river on stepping stones, climb up the sides of houses, slide down chimneys and so on. (PD1, 2, 3, 6)

CREATIVE DEVELOPMENT

- Play the card spotting game (see activity opposite). (C3)

ACTIVITY: Card puzzle game MD.

Learning opportunity: Recognising matching shapes and rebuilding cards.

Early Learning Goal: Mathematical Development. Children will talk about, recognise and recreate simple patterns. They will solve practical problems.

Resources: A selection of interesting Christmas cards.

Organisation: Small group.

Key vocabulary: Same, different, match, pair, two.

WHAT TO DO:

Cut each Christmas card in half using clear but distinctive lines.

Spread six of the cards (12 halves) on the table top, face up. Talk to the children about how you have prepared the game. Show them both halves of one of the cards.

Explain that now the pieces have become all muddled up. Can they help you to find the 'partners'? What clues could they look for? Point out the pictures on the card and the shape of the cut lines.

The game can be made more difficult by adding more cards to the collection or by turning them face down before children try to find the matching halves.

ACTIVITY: Card spotting game CD.

Learning opportunity: Describing Christmas card pictures and identifying cards from given descriptions.

Early Learning Goal: Creative Development. Children will respond in a variety of ways to what they see and hear.

Resources: Ten Christmas cards with clear pictures, including pairs on a similar theme.

Organisation: Six children seated around a large table or in a circle on the floor. (This may be played with the whole group but works best with small groups.)

Key vocabulary: Robin, snowman, holly, tree, bauble.

WHAT TO DO:

Show the group the cards. Ask general questions about the pictures to help focus attention on their detail. How many robins can you see? What decorations are on the trees? What is the snowman wearing?

Explain that you are going to play a game in which someone describes a card and everyone else has to guess which the card is. Give the children one clue to a card for example, 'The card I have chosen has a robin on it'. Ask the group which cards fit this description. Give another clue and again see if cards can be eliminated. Continue until the card has been identified.

Repeat the activity but this time ask children to put up their hand when they think they know which card has been chosen. Finally, invite children to take it in turns to describe a card for the group to identify.

DISPLAY

Make a display of sets of sorted Christmas cards: a set of cards with robins, a set of cards with Father Christmas, and so on. Encourage children to make their own cards to add to each set.

DAYS 9 AND 10

CHRISTMAS PRESENTS

PERSONAL, SOCIAL AND EMOTIONAL DEVELOPMENT

- Read *The Big Sneeze* by HE Todd and Val Biro (Knight Books) or a similar story in which presents are given. Talk about the types of presents children like to receive. Discuss what would be appropriate presents for the characters in children's favourite stories. (PS2)

LANGUAGE AND LITERACY

- Cut out paper stockings and ask children to make Christmas present lists on them for a nursery rhyme character by writing, drawing or sticking pictures from magazines/catalogues. (L16, 18)

- Place a variety of objects in a sack which children might receive in stockings. Ask children to feel and describe a present. Can other children identify the present from the description? (L1)

- Play 'In Santa's sack there is a ......' In turn children say the list and add one more gift. The game ends when children are unable to remember the total list in order. (L1)

MATHEMATICAL DEVELOPMENT

- Paste four A4 pieces of wrapping paper onto card. From each cut a number of playing cards in distinct 2D shapes: a star, a circle, a square, an oblong, a triangle. Stick a picture of a toy on the other side of each card. Spread the cards and invite children to guess 'What do you think is under the red square/silver star?' and so on. As children identify the correct shape they turn it over to discover the surprise. (M9)

- Printing wrapping paper. Provide a range of small printing blocks. Show the children some wrapping paper and point out the patterns. Encourage the children to print their own paper. Talk about making repeating patterns using shapes and colours. How do we know which shape or colour comes next in the pattern? (M8)

KNOWLEDGE AND UNDERSTANDING OF THE WORLD

- Do some bead printing. Take a deep-sided seed tray and line it with paper. Provide margarine tubs containing ready-mixed paint. Place a large wooden bead in each tub. Children use teaspoons to transfer the paint-covered bead to the tray. By tipping the tray and allowing the bead to roll over it they leave a paint trail on the paper. Talk about how the bead can be made to stop or change direction. Change beads to add new colours. Dry results can be used for wrapping paper. (K4)

- Make balancing Santas (see activity opposite). (K4)

PHYSICAL DEVELOPMENT

- Mime being a present being unopened. (PD1, 2)

- Practise aiming bean bags into different shaped boxes covered with wrapping paper. (PD6)

CREATIVE DEVELOPMENT

- Open the box activity (see activity opposite). (C4)

- Make collage parcels. For each child fold a piece of A2 paper in half and cut into a parcel shape. Show children how to open the paper and to draw or paint a picture of what they would like to find in a parcel. Now close the paper and 'wrap' the parcel using a collage of wrapping paper scraps, parcel ribbon and sequins. (C1)

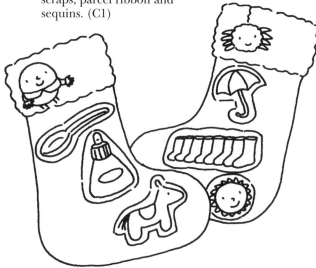

ACTIVITY: Balancing Santas

KUW.

Learning opportunity: Making a balancing toy and discussing how it might work.

Early Learning Goal: Knowledge and Understanding of the World. Children will ask questions about why things happen and how things work.

Resources: A pre-drawn Santa on stiff card and two one pence coins for each child; wax crayons; pencils; sticky tape; scissors; a completed balancing Santa.

Organisation: Small group of up to six children.

Key vocabulary: Balance, topple, stand-up, fall over.

WHAT TO DO:

Explain that the children are going to make balancing Santas. Show the children one made already and how it can balance on the end of a finger.

Next show the children a Santa without coins attached to the hands. Demonstrate that it will not balance. Ask children what is the difference between the two Santas. Encourage children to talk about things that balance. How do they balance when walking across a beam or standing on one leg?

Provide each child with a Santa and ask them to decorate them. It is best to use pencil or wax crayons - felt pens can make the card too soggy to balance.

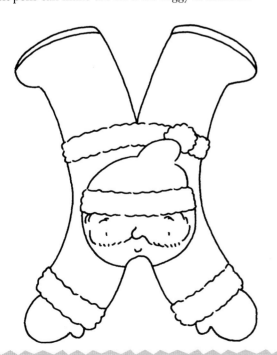

ACTIVITY: Open the box

CD.

Learning opportunity: Using and interpreting imaginative mime.

Early Learning Goal: Creative Development. Children will use their imagination.

Resources: An empty lidded box - perhaps covered in wrapping paper.

Organisation: Large group sitting in circle.

WHAT TO DO:

Sit with the group. Show the children the box and explain that inside the box is a very special gift. Slowly remove the box and describe what is in there, without saying what it is, for example, 'It is very soft and furry. I think I would like to cuddle this. It has two arms and two legs, a round tummy and a friendly face.' Pretend to lift the present out of the box and to mime how you would hold it, or what you would do with it. Examples to use are a teddy, a box of paints, a ball.

Encourage the children to guess what it was that you found in the box, and then pass the box to the child next to you. What will she find in it? Perhaps it will be the same present as yours or perhaps it will be something quite different!

Play the activity during several days so that eventually all the children have had a turn. The concentration involved in playing it well is too intense for children to sustain for more than a few minutes, but produced as a five-minute treat during a few days it is a real winner!

DISPLAY

Make a display of the wrapping papers designed by the children. Incorporate words which describe the shapes and colours they have used. Intersperse with parcel bows and ribbons.

DAYS 11 AND 12

THE CHRISTMAS PARTY

PERSONAL, SOCIAL AND EMOTIONAL DEVELOPMENT

- Talk about the forthcoming Christmas party. Discuss the importance of looking after each other at the party to ensure that everyone has an enjoyable time. (PS8)

- As the children work together towards the event, encourage the idea of taking responsibility for small aspects of the preparation and the idea of collaboration. (PS8)

LANGUAGE AND LITERACY

- Read *The Naughtiest Story of All* in *My Naughty Little Sister* by Dorothy Edwards (Puffin). (L3)

- Play 'I -Spy with my Christmas eye....' (L1, 11)

MATHEMATICAL DEVELOPMENT

- Adapt counting songs for Christmas, for example to the tune of 'Ten Green Bottles' sing:

  'Ten red crackers for a Christmas tea, ten red crackers for a Christmas tea,

  And if one red cracker should be pulled by you and me,

  There'll be nine red crackers for the Christmas tea.' (M1)

- Play the star game (see activity opposite). (M1, 3)

KNOWLEDGE AND UNDERSTANDING OF THE WORLD

- Make Christmas decoration biscuits (see activity opposite). (K1)

PHYSICAL DEVELOPMENT

- Practise movement games for the party such as musical statues or ring games. (PD1, 2, 3)

CREATIVE DEVELOPMENT

- Make paper chain decorations using different matt and shiny paper in different colours. (C1)

- Complete the decoration of the tree by making paper lanterns from foil paper (see below), fir cones dipped in glue and then glitter, and foil shapes decorated with sequins. (C1, 4)

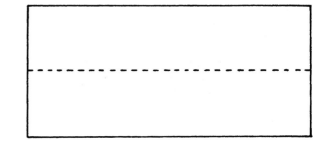

fold

cuts

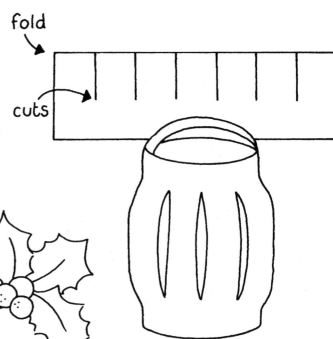

ACTIVITY: The star game MD.

Learning opportunity: Recognising numbers within the context of a game.

Early Learning Goal: Mathematical Development. Children will recognise numerals to six. They will say and use number names in order.

Resources: Two large dice; about 20 A5-size stars cut from card.

Organisation: Whole group seated in a circle on the floor in an area where it is safe to run. The stars are placed in the centre.

Key vocabulary: Numbers one to six.

WHAT TO DO:

Explain that the group is going to play a game. In turn children roll the dice. If they throw a double they shout 'star!', run around the outside of the circle in a clockwise direction, come in through their place to the centre, pick up a star and return to their place. However, the throwing of the dice continues while they are running and if someone else has shouted star before they have had a chance to pick up a star they return to their place immediately without collecting a star. The winner is the one who collects the most stars. Other versions of the game can use one die and children only run when they throw a six.

ACTIVITY: Christmas decoration biscuits KUW.

Learning opportunity: Exploring materials and using skills through decorating biscuits.

Early Learning Goal: Knowledge and Understanding of the World. Children will investigate materials.

Resources: Coconut ring biscuits; ribbons; icing sugar; food colouring; assorted sugar decorations or tiny sweets; teaspoons; small bowls; table covers; aprons; hand-washing resources.

Organisation: Small group.

Key vocabulary: Powder, dry, moist, sticky, soft, hard.

WHAT TO DO:

Explain to the children that they are going to be working with food. Talk about the need for hygiene and careful hand-washing.

Show the children the icing sugar in the packet. Talk about how it looks and feels. Make up the icing with water following packet instructions. Encourage the children to describe the changes they observe. Add food colouring if desired, pointing out how only a tiny drop of colour makes a great difference to the colour of the icing.

Supply each child with a coconut ring biscuit. Explain the need for gentle handling as the biscuits will break fairly easily.

Show the children how to use a teaspoon to dribble icing around a biscuit ring, and then allow a free choice of decorations. Explain that it is important to put the decorations on the biscuit before the icing sets!

Finally, thread a piece of narrow ribbon through the biscuit ring so that it can be hung as a decoration at home.

DISPLAY

Make a 'Getting ready for the party' display with examples of all the children's preparations.

BRINGING IT ALL TOGETHER

THE CHRISTMAS PARTY

Talk to the children about Christmas parties. What makes a successful party? Some children may have been to parties with professional entertainers. Explain to children that this is a special party. They are going to help organise it and to plan their own entertainment!

Ask them to make suggestions about games to play, favourite songs and party foods.

It can be a good idea to incorporate the making of accessories into the party itself. This allows alternation of quiet/noisy times. These activities can also be used to keep children happily occupied at one end of the hall while other adults are busy at the other, for example, putting food out.

FOOD

Involve the children in preparing the party food:

- Thread hoop-shaped potato snacks on thread or string to make edible bracelets.

- Cut sandwiches or pizza slices using shaped cutters, especially stars and Christmas trees.

- Freeze fruit juices in ice cube containers of Christmas shapes to add to party drinks.

- Use icing and sugar decorations to make chocolate rolls or small cakes look like parcels.

GAMES

Most of the following are variations on familiar ideas:

- Pin the star on the tree, or the nose on Rudolph. Use a blob of Blu-tack rather than a pin and be aware that some young children dislike blindfolds.

- Make a magnetic parcel fishing game. Fasten magnets on a string to rulers or short sticks to make fishing rods. Cut out parcel shapes from paper-covered card and fix a paper-clip to each. On each parcel write an instruction of something for the whole group to do, for example, jump ten times, pat their heads and rub their tummies, sing a nursery rhyme. This will help to keep everyone interested as the children take turns to 'fish'.

- Musical Christmas miming. Each time the music stops, ask the children to mime a different Christmas activity - unwrapping parcels, eating a mince pie, decorating the tree, a reindeer pulling Santa's sleigh.

- Play 'Here we go round the Christmas tree' to the tune of 'Here we go round the mulberry bush', changing the words of verses to allow actions similar to those of Christmas miming (above).

ACCESSORIES TO MAKE

- Party hats:
  Provide pre-cut paper strips with one edge cut in 'crown' zig-zags and several glue sticks. Allow children totally free use of a selection of decorative materials - gummed shapes, sequins, cut foil shapes, paper curls.

- Drinking straw decorations:
  Using templates or old Christmas cards show children how to cut out and decorate Christmas shapes. Make small slits at the top and bottom of the shapes and thread a plastic straw through to make personalised designs. Plastic or paper party cups can be decorated to match.

- Party bags:
  If you are going to provide small 'going home' treats, supply small paper bags which children can name and decorate.

SONGS

Invite collecting adults to arrive a few minutes early to share a Christmas sing-a-long before taking children home.

'When Santa got stuck in the chimney'

'Rudolph the Red-Nosed Reindeer'

'Jingle Bells'

STORIES

- *Lucy and Tom's Christmas* by Shirley Hughes (Puffin Books).

- *A Bear for Christmas* by Holly Keller (Hippo Books).

- *Mog's Christmas* by Judith Kerr (Picture Lions).

RESOURCES

RESOURCES TO COLLECT

- Christmas trimmings, wrapping papers, parcel bows, old Christmas cards.
- Nativity figures to use for display and to illustrate the Christmas story.

EVERYDAY RESOURCES

- Boxes, large and small for modelling.
- Papers and cards of different weights, colours and textures.
- Dry powder paints for mixing and mixed paints for covering large areas such as card tree trunks.
- Different-sized paint brushes from household brushes to thin brushes for delicate work and a variety of paint mixing containers.
- A variety of drawing and colouring pencils, crayons, pastels, charcoals.
- Additional decorative and finishing materials such as sequins, foils, glitter, tinsel, shiny wool and threads, beads, pieces of textiles, ribbon.
- Table covers.

STORIES

The Jolly Christmas Postman by Janet and Allan Ahlberg (Heinemann).

Jesus' Christmas Party by Nicholas Allan (Hutchinson).

The First Christmas retold by Lynne Bradbury (Ladybird).

The Snowman by Raymond Briggs (Ladybird).

Paddington's Magical Christmas by Michael Bond (Collins).

The Nativity Play by Nick Butterworth and Mick Inkpen (Picture Knight).

'The Naughtiest Story of All' in *My Naughty Little Sister* by Dorothy Edwards (Puffin).

Lucy and Tom's Christmas by Shirley Hughes (Puffin Books).

Mrs Christmas by Penny Ives (Hamish Hamilton).

A Bear for Christmas by Holly Keller (Hippo Books).

Mog's Christmas by Judith Kerr (Picture Lions).

The Little Christ Child and the Spiders by Jan Peters (Macdonald).

The Big Sneeze by H E Todd and Val Biro (Knight Books).

Kipper's Christmas Eve by Mick Inkpen (Hodder Children's Books).

A Message for Santa by Hiawyn Oram and Tony Ross (Collins Picture Lions).

Little Angel by Geraldine McCaughrean and Ian Beck (Orchard Picture Books).

A Letter to Father Christmas by Rose Impey and Sue Porter (Orchard Picture Books).

Sssh! by Julie Sykes and Tim Warnes (Magi Publications).

Hurry Santa! by Julie Sykes and Tim Warnes (Magi Publications).

Little Robin Red Vest by Jan Fearnley (Methuen).

FOR OLDER CHILDREN

Josie Smith at Christmas by Magdalen Nabb (Young Lion Storybook).

'Mrs Lily's Christmas Story' (Issue 6, *Practical Pre-school*)

POEMS

This Little Puffin by Elizabeth Matterson (Puffin).

Out and About by Shirley Hughes (Walker Books).

A Single Star - an anthology of Christmas poetry compiled by David Davies (Puffin).

The Puffin Book of Christmas Poems compiled by Wes Magee (Puffin Books).

COLLECTING EVIDENCE OF CHILDREN'S LEARNING

Monitoring children's development is an important task. Keeping a record of children's achievements will help you to see progress and will draw attention to those who are having difficulties for some reason. If a child needs additional professional help, such as speech therapy, your records will provide valuable evidence.

Records should be the result of collaboration between group leaders, parents and carers. Parents should be made aware of your record keeping policies when their child joins your group. Show them the type of records you are keeping and make sure they understand that they have an opportunity to contribute. As a general rule, your records should form an open document. Any parent should have access to records relating to his or her child. Take regular opportunities to talk to parents about children's progress. If you have formal discussions regarding children about whom you have particular concerns, a dated record of the main points should be kept.

KEEPING IT MANAGEABLE

Records should be helpful in informing group leaders, adult helpers and parents and always be for the benefit of the child. However, keeping records of every aspect of each child's development can become a difficult task. The sample shown will help to keep records manageable and useful. The golden rule is to keep them simple.

Observations will basically fall into three categories:

- **Spontaneous records:** Sometimes you will want to make a note of observations as they happen, for example, a child is heard counting cars accurately during a play activity, or is seen to play collaboratively for the first time.

- **Planned observations:** Sometimes you will plan to make observations of children's developing skills in their everyday activities. Using the learning opportunity identified for an activity will help you to make appropriate judgements about children's capabilities and to record them systematically.

To collect information:

- talk to children about their activities and listen to their responses;

- listen to children talking to each other;

- observe children's work such as early writing, drawings, paintings and 3-D models. Keeping photocopies or photographs is sometimes useful.

Sometimes you may wish to set up 'one off' activities for the purposes of monitoring development. Some groups, for example, ask children to make a drawing of themselves at the beginning of each term to record their progressing skills in both co-ordination and observation. Do not attempt to make records following every activity!

- **Reflective observations:** It is useful to spend regular time reflecting on the progress of a few children (about four children each week). Aim to make some brief comments about each child every half term.

INFORMING YOUR PLANNING

Collecting evidence about children's progress is time consuming and it is important that it is useful. When you are planning, use the information you have collected to help you to decide what learning opportunities you need to provide next for children. For example, a child who has poor pencil or brush control will benefit from more play with dough or construction toys to build the strength of hand muscles.

Example of recording chart

Name: Lucy Copson		D.O.B. 26.2.97		Date of entry: 13.9.00	
Term	**Personal, Social and Emotional**	**Language and Literacy**	**Mathematical Development**	**Knowledge and Understanding**	**Physical Development**	**Creative Development**
ONE	Enjoyed making a card for her family 15.12.00 EMH	Wrote first three letters of name independently on Christmas card 15.12.00 EMH	Is able to say numbers to ten and to count accurately five objects. Recognises and names squares and circles. 5.11.00 BM	Very keen on minibeasts Brought in pictures from home. 16.10.00 AC	Can balance on one leg. Finds threading beads difficult. 16.10.00 AC	Enjoys gluing and cutting. Made a wonderful Duplo castle 20.10.00 LSS
TWO						
THREE						

SKILLS OVERVIEW OF TWELVE-DAY PLAN CHRISTMAS

Days	Topic focus	Personal, Social and Emotional Development	Language and Literacy	Mathematical Development	Knowledge and Understanding of the World	Physical Development	Creative Development
1/2	Advent	Sensitivity to others	Developing vocabulary Role play	Counting	Making observations	Moving imaginatively	Drawing Cutting
3/4	Christmas decorations	Appreciation Sensitivity to others	Listening to stories Initial sounds	Describing size and shape Repeating patterns	Making observations Sorting	Miming Controlling movement	Working in three dimensions Cutting and gluing
5/6	Christmas story	Talking about feelings	Re-telling stories Role play	Ordering numbers	Recording observations Environmental awareness	Controlling movement	Singing Cutting and gluing
7/8	Christmas cards	Working collaboratively	Describing Word awareness	Sorting by shape Matching	Choosing materials	Climbing	Describing
9/10	Christmas presents	Sensitivity to others	Describing	Identifying shapes Making and continuing patterns	Describing observations	Miming Aiming	Role play Collage
11/12	Christmas party	Sharing responsibility	Initial sounds Listening to stories	Counting Recognising numbers	Selecting and using materials	Moving confidently	Using materials Cutting and joining

HOME LINKS

The theme of Christmas lends itself to useful links with children's homes and families. Through working together children and adults gain respect for each other and build comfortable and confident relationships.

ESTABLISHING PARTNERSHIPS

- Keep parents informed about the topic of Christmas and the themes for each day. By understanding the work of the group, parents will enjoy the involvement of contributing ideas, time and resources.

- Photocopy the parent's page for each child to take home.

- Invite friends, childminders and families to share all or part of the Christmas party.

VISITING ENTHUSIASTS

- Invite adults to come to the group to share their childhood memories of Christmas. Some may be prepared to bring objects associated with Christmas to show to the children.

RESOURCE REQUESTS

- Ask parents to contribute any Christmas trimmings or decorations which are no longer needed. Parcel bows, Christmas wrapping papers and old Christmas cards will all be valuable. It is worth continuing to collect these after Christmas to save for next year.

PREPARING THE PARTY

- If the children are to be involved in helping to prepare food, they will need extra support. Any additional help would be of great value.

- Put out a party suggestion box in which parents can contribute ideas for successful games or activities.

- Invite parents to request favourite Christmas songs at the end of party sing-a-long.